Creative Crafts for Kids

Valentine CRAFTS

By Greta Speechley

Gareth Stevens
Publishing

Please visit our Web site www.garethstevens.com. For a free color catalog of all our high-quality books, call toll free 1-800-542-2595 or fax 1-877-542-2596.

Library of Congress Cataloging-in-Publication Data
Speechley, Greta, 1948-
    Valentine crafts / Greta Speechley.
        p. cm. — (Creative crafts for kids)
    Includes index.
    ISBN 978-1-4339-3600-5 (library binding)
    ISBN 978-1-4339-3598-5 (pbk.)
    ISBN 978-1-4339-3599-2 (6-pack)
    1. Valentine decorations—Juvenile literature. 2. Handicraft—Juvenile literature. I. Title.
    TT900.V34S64 2010
    745.594'1—dc22
                                                            2009039324

Published in 2010 by
Gareth Stevens Publishing
111 East 14th Street, Suite 349
New York, NY 10003

© 2010 The Brown Reference Group Ltd.

For Gareth Stevens Publishing:
Art Direction: Haley Harasymiw
Editorial Direction: Kerri O'Donnell

For The Brown Reference Group Ltd:
Editorial Director: Lindsey Lowe
Managing Editor: Tim Harris
Children's Publisher: Anne O'Daly
Design Manager: David Poole
Production Director: Alastair Gourlay

Picture Credits:
All photographs: Martin Norris
Front Cover: Shutterstock: Rachel Burnside and Martin Norris

Manufactured in the United States of America
1 2 3 4 5 6 7 8 9 12 11 10

CPSIA compliance information: Batch #BRW0102GS: For further information contact Gareth Stevens, New York, New York at 1-800-542-2595.

Contents

Introduction 4

Spinning valentine 6

Kiss seal 8

Fortuneteller 10

Love bugs 12

Lip smackers 14

Lovebird 16

Red rose 18

Broken heart jigsaw 20

Lavender heart 22

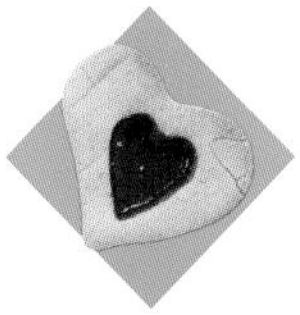

Heart cookies 24

Keepsakes 26

Chocolate lollipops 28

Patterns 30

Glossary and Index 32

Introduction

This book is packed with projects for Valentine's Day. Try making our clever card with a wheel that turns, and then seal the envelope with a loving kiss stamp! There are chocolate lollipops and love bugs to make for your friends. If February is a long way off, a keepsake or scented cushion would make a touching gift at any time of the year.

YOU WILL NEED

Each project includes a list of all the things you need.

Before you buy new materials, look around at home to see what you could use instead. For example, you can cut cardboard shapes out of empty cereal boxes.

To make the red rose and the keepsakes, we have used special florist's wire, tape, and fabric stamens. You can buy them from a flower store. To make the heart cushion, you will need to buy dried lavender from a department store.

Getting started

Read the steps for the project first.

Gather together all the items you need.

Cover your work surface with newspaper.

Wear an apron, or change into old clothes.

A message for adults

All the projects in Valentine Crafts have been designed for children to make, but occasionally they will need you to help. Some of the projects do require the use of sharp utensils, such as scissors or needles. Please read the instructions before your child starts work.

Making patterns

Follow these steps to make the patterns on pages 30 and 31. Using a pencil, trace the pattern onto tracing paper. If you're making a project out of fabric, you can cut out the tracing paper pattern and pin it onto the fabric. To cut the pattern out of cardboard, turn the tracing over, and lay it onto the cardboard. Rub firmly over the pattern with a pencil. The shape will appear on the cardboard. Cut out the shape.

When you have finished

Wash paintbrushes, and put everything away.

Put pens, pencils, paints, and glue in an old box or ice-cream container.

Keep scissors and any other sharp items in a safe place.

Stick needles and pins into a pincushion or a piece of scrap cloth.

BE SAFE

Look out for the safety boxes. They will appear whenever you need to ask an adult for help.

Ask an adult to help you use sharp scissors.

Spinning valentine

Make a Valentine card with a moving wheel. When you turn the wheel, a tiny picture or a written message appears in the window.

YOU WILL NEED

thin white cardboard 12in x 6in (30cm x 15cm)	colored paper in four colors
	red shiny paper
tracing paper	gold and red glitter pens
pencil	paper glue
paper fastener	stickers or a paper stamp
yellow cardboard	compass
pinking shears	ruler
scissors	

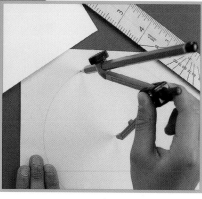

1 Fold the white cardboard in half to make a square. Draw a circle with a diameter of 5in (12.5cm) onto yellow cardboard using a compass. Cut out the circle using pinking shears; this will be a wheel.

6

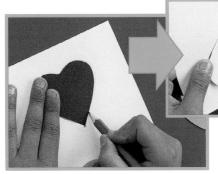

2 Open the card, and place the wheel on the inside of the front cover, sticking out at the side. Push the compass needle into the center of the circle so that it goes through the white card, too.

3 Trace the heart on page 30. Transfer the tracing onto colored paper, and cut out the heart. Make three more hearts in different colors. Place a heart on the front of the card so that the tip is in line with the hole. Draw around the heart, and cut it out to make a window.

4 Glue the colored hearts to the yellow wheel with their tips at the center, and decorate each heart with small Valentine stickers or paper stamps. You could write a message on each heart as well.

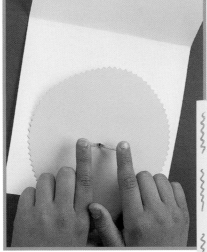

5 Decorate the front of the card with squiggles using glitter pens and hearts cut out of red shiny paper.

6 Fix the wheel to the inside of the front of the card with a paper fastener, so the hearts show through the hole.

Kiss seal

When you're ready to send your Valentine card, make an envelope and seal it with a kiss.

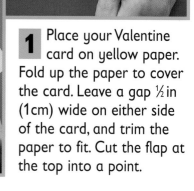

1 Place your Valentine card on yellow paper. Fold up the paper to cover the card. Leave a gap ½ in (1cm) wide on either side of the card, and trim the paper to fit. Cut the flap at the top into a point.

8

2 Stick the sides of the envelope together using double-sided tape. Decorate the front of the card with glitter pens, and glue on hearts cut out from shiny red paper.

3 To make sponge stamps, draw lips or a heart onto a kitchen sponge. Cut out the shapes. For our lips, we have cut out the top lip and the bottom lip separately.

4 Glue the sponge shapes onto squares of thick, corrugated cardboard. Let the glue dry.

5 Glue a plastic bottle top onto the back of the cardboard to act as a handle for your stamp.

6 Put the Valentine card into the envelope and seal the envelope with tape or glue. Dab red paint onto the sponge stamp using a paintbrush. Press the stamp down on the back of the envelope.

Fortuneteller

By folding paper in clever ways, you can make a simple fortunetelling game. Write initials in the middle so that the final fortune tells you the first letter of your true love's name!

YOU WILL NEED

square piece of colored paper about 10in x 10in (25cm x 25cm)

felt-tip pens

1 Fold the piece of paper in half and then in half again to make a small square.

2 Open out the paper. Now fold each corner into the center. You can see where the center of the paper is because it is marked by the folds you made before.

10

3 Turn over the square, and fold the corners into the center again. Now open out the fortuneteller so that you can decorate it.

4 Draw a heart in each of the four corner squares using felt-tip pens. These are the squares you will see when the fortuneteller is pinched closed.

5 Now decorate the triangles on either side of the colored hearts. Write the numbers from 1 to 8 on each triangle. You may need to refold the fortuneteller to make sure the numbers are the right way up.

6 Draw hearts on the center squares, and write a letter or a short fortune in each. To use the fortuneteller, fold it up and hold it pinched between your first fingers and thumbs. Ask a friend to choose a number from 1 to 8. Pinch the fortuneteller open, forward, and then sideways that number of times. Read off the number, and pinch again. Lift up the flap to read the fortune.

11

Love bugs

Make these critters for Valentine's Day using your favorite cookies and cakes. But be careful you don't get bitten by a love bug!

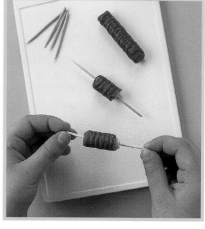

YOU WILL NEED

5 toothpicks	rice paper
cake roll	scissors
chocolate tea cake	red writing icing
2 chocolate fingers	2 round candies
marshmallows	

1 To make legs for a love bug, first cut or snap two chocolate finger cookies in half. Then cut four toothpicks in half, and push a piece of toothpick into each end of each piece of finger cookie.

12

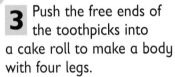

2 Push a marshmallow onto each leg to make a squashy bug foot.

3 Push the free ends of the toothpicks into a cake roll to make a body with four legs.

4 Cut another toothpick in half, and push it into a tea cake. This is the head. Push the head onto one end of the body. Use writing icing to stick on two candies for eyes.

5 Cut out a heart from rice paper. Stick it onto the bug's back using writing icing, and decorate it with red, iced hearts.

Eat your love bug carefully, leg by leg, and don't eat the toothpicks.

Lip smackers

Steal a kiss with these huge, glossy lips! The grabber contraption is easy to make and great fun to play with.

YOU WILL NEED

stiff cardboard or foam board, 10in x 10in (25cm x 25cm)

scissors

ruler

pencil

7 paper fasteners

shiny red cardboard

double-sided tape

1 Use the width of your ruler to mark out 6 strips on the foam board; each should be 10in (25cm) long. Make crosses half way along each strip lengthwise. Make crosses at one end of each strip about ½in (1cm) from the end. On two of the strips make a cross at the other end, ½in (1cm) in. Look at the diagram (left) to help you.

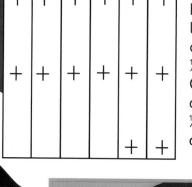

2 Cut out the six strips. Use a pencil to make holes where you have marked a cross.

14

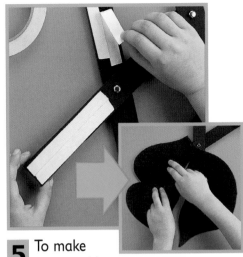

3 Pick up the two strips that have three holes in them and make a cross. Push a paper fastener through the center hole, and press out the fastener arms on the other side.

4 Make two more crosses with the other strips. Then attach these two crosses on either side of the first cross so that the points without holes are at the ends.

5 To make your grabber stretch out, push two ends (the handles) together. Stick double-sided tape to the two points at the other end. Cut out a bottom lip and a top lip from shiny red cardboard, and stick them to the tape so that the lips are closed. When you pull the handles apart, the lips will open. Pucker up!

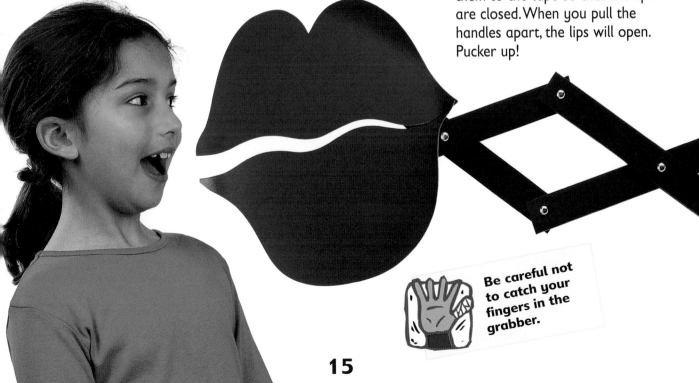

Be careful not to catch your fingers in the grabber.

Lovebird

This beautiful bird with rainbow feathers can carry a tiny card in its beak. It is a lovely project to make for February 14.

YOU WILL NEED

plastic bottle	scrap white paper
polystyrene ball	scraps of colored felt
pipe cleaners	6 bendy straws
orange, purple, green, and red paper	tape and glue
scissors	double-sided tape
felt-tip pen	yellow cardboard
tracing paper	
pencil	

1 To make the head and body of your lovebird, glue a polystyrene ball into the neck of a bottle.

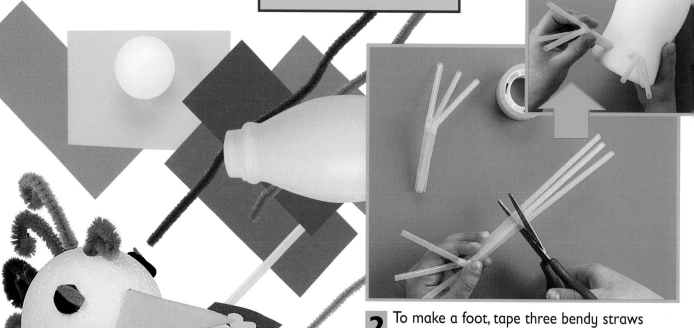

2 To make a foot, tape three bendy straws together, then cut off the ends. Make another foot. Ask an adult to cut two holes in the bottle near the bottom. Push the feet into the holes.

3 Trace the wing and feather patterns on pages 30 and 31. Transfer the tracings onto paper, following the instructions on page 5. Cut out the shapes. Draw around these paper templates onto colored paper. (The color is noted on each pattern.) If it is a half pattern, fold the colored paper, and line up the straight edge of the template with the fold. Draw around the template, and cut out the shape.

Ask an adult to cut two holes in the bottom of the bottle for the bird's legs.

4 Slot the purple feather piece over the bird's body. Now stick one orange wing to each side with double-sided tape. Glue the green tail feathers to the bird's back, and tape the collar of red feathers around its neck.

5 Cut out two eyes, a jagged collar, and pink hearts from felt. Glue them onto the bird.

6 Use the beak half pattern on page 31 to cut out an upper beak from yellow cardboard. Make a lower beak as well. Glue the beak tabs to the bird's head. Push pieces of curled-up pipe cleaner into the head to make a crest.

17

Red rose

Make a single red rose for
someone close to your heart.
To make the stem, we have
used florist's wire and tape.
You can buy them from
a flower store.

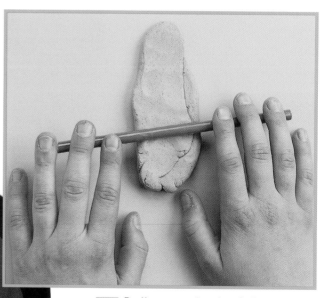

1 Roll out a chunk of clay using
a round pencil or a rolling pin.
The clay should be about ¼in
(0.5cm) thick.

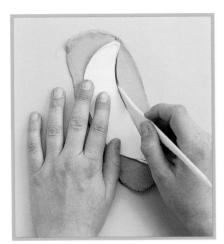

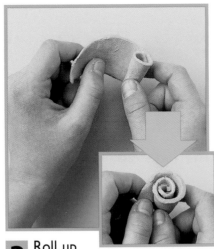

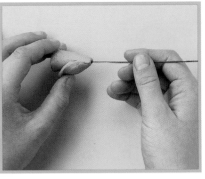

2 Trace the pattern on page 30. Transfer the shape onto paper, following the instructions on page 5, and cut it out. Place the paper pattern on the clay, and cut around it using a clay cutter.

3 Roll up the clay, squeezing it in slightly at the base. Ease out the top edges to make petals.

4 Push the florist's wire into the rose and pull it out, to make a hole. Ask an adult to bake the rose, following the instructions on the clay package. Let it cool, and then glue the wire into the hole in the rose.

Ask an adult to help you bake the clay rose.

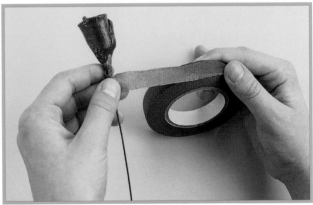

5 Paint the rose using red poster paint. Let the paint dry. Varnish the flower using clay varnish. We have used sparkly varnish.

6 Wrap the base of the rose and the top of the stem with green florist's tape. This type of tape doesn't feel sticky, but it will stay in place without glue. Wrap the rose in cellophane to make it look extra special. Tie a ribbon around the stem. You could thread a paper label with a message onto the ribbon if you like.

Broken heart jigsaw

A cardboard jigsaw like this one makes a great mystery gift. Your valentine has to piece together the jigsaw to mend the broken heart.

YOU WILL NEED

pencil	gold wrapping paper
white cardboard	glue
tracing paper	fabric rose
scissors	red felt
felt-tip pens	gold fabric pen
large matchbox	

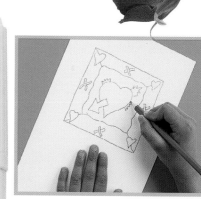

1 Trace the heart-and-arrow design on page 30. Turn over the tracing and transfer it onto white cardboard, following the instructions on page 5.

2 Color in the design using felt-tip pens. Go over the pencil lines with a black felt-tip pen to make the design look bold. Cut out the picture.

3 Turn over the picture, and write your message on the card. Remember: You're not supposed to sign your name on a Valentine's card. We've simply signed ours "?"—from a secret admirer!

4 Cut the card into five or six pieces to make a jigsaw. Don't cut it up into too many pieces, though, or your valentine won't be able to mend the broken heart.

5 To make a gift box for the jigsaw pieces, wrap gold paper around a large matchbox. Glue a fabric rose to the top. Cut out a heart from red felt, and draw on a gold outline with a fabric pen. Glue the heart onto the box to cover the stem of the rose.

Lavender heart

Make a beautiful scented cushion for someone on Valentine's Day. Your lucky valentine can hang the cushion by their bed or in the closet.

YOU WILL NEED

scrap paper	lavender
pencil	gold fabric pen
black felt	
dark red velvety fabric	scrap of shiny fabric
needle and thread	plastic gems
	pins
dark red ribbon	scissors
heart bead	gold tassel
cotton wool	fabric glue

1 Draw a heart onto scrap paper. Make the heart a bit bigger than the size of your outspread hand. Cut it out, and pin it to the red velvet. Cut around the paper to make a velvet heart.

22

2 To make the back of the cushion, fold the paper heart in half. Pin the heart to two pieces of felt so that the paper fold is ½in (1cm) away from the edges. Cut around the curved part of the heart, and then cut out to the edges of the felt.

3 Pin the two pieces of felt to the velvety side of the red fabric heart so that the flaps of felt overlap at the center. Sew around the pinned edge, taking out the pins as you go.

4 Turn the heart inside out. Stuff it with cotton wool, and add 1 tablespoon of lavender. Sew the edges of felt together along the center seam.

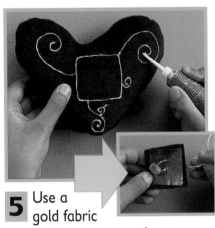

5 Use a gold fabric pen to draw a square frame onto the heart. Cut out a square of black felt smaller than the gold frame and a slightly smaller square of shiny fabric. Place the shiny square on top of the felt square. Sew a heart-shaped bead to the center, and sew the little pile to the cushion.

6 Glue on some plastic gems. To finish, sew a loop of ribbon to the top and a gold tassel to the bottom. Your heart is ready to hang up.

Heart cookies

Make these cute heart cookies with their little windows. The stained-glass centers are made from crushed hard candies.

YOU WILL NEED

package of ready-made cookie mix	plain flour
mixing bowl	baking tray
fork and spoon	red, orange, and yellow hard candies
one large and one small heart-shaped cookie cutter	rolling pin
rice paper	small food bag
	chopping board

1 Pour the cookie mix into a bowl, and add water, following the instructions on the cookie package. Stir the mixture using a fork until it becomes a dough and you can make it into a ball with your hands.

2 Sprinkle flour onto a clean kitchen surface or a sheet of baking paper. Rub flour over your rolling pin, too. Roll out the dough until it is about ¼in (0.5cm) thick.

24

3 Cut out hearts from the dough using the large cookie cutter. Put the cutter in position, and press down, then carefully ease the heart out of the cutter.

4 Press the small cookie cutter into the center of each heart to cut out a small window. Then collect all the extra bits of dough and small hearts, and make it into a ball. Roll it out again so you can make a few more cookies.

5 Unwrap a handful of hard candies, and put them all into a plastic bag. Tie a knot in the bag. Bash the candies with a rolling pin to break them up. It is best to do this on a chopping board.

Ask an adult to bake the heart cookies for you.

6 Line a baking tray with edible rice paper. Place the cookies onto the tray, and spoon the broken candies into the little heart windows. Ask an adult to bake the cookies in the oven for you, following the instructions on the cookie mix package.

Keepsakes

These delicate fabric hearts are treasures to keep or to give as gifts. You can make them into pendants, brooches, or hair barrettes—just follow these steps.

YOU WILL NEED

red felt	clear glue
felt-tip pen	fabric glue
scissors	plastic gems
cardboard	brooch back
fabric stamens from a flower store, or strands of silver tinsel	gold thread

1 Draw a small heart onto cardboard, and cut it out. Draw around the cardboard template onto red felt. Cut out the red felt heart.

2 Bend a few florist's stamens in half, and glue them to the center of the cardboard heart so the ends stick out around the edge. If you don't have florist's stamens, use strands of tinsel, or glue on tiny cardboard wings.

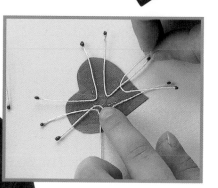

26

3 Glue the red felt heart on top of the cardboard heart.

4 Glue a brooch back to the cardboard side of the little heart. Let the glue dry.

HANDY HINT

To make a pendant, glue a loop of gold thread to the back of the keepsake. You can make a Valentine decoration for your hair, too, by gluing a heart or a row of hearts to the top of a barrette.

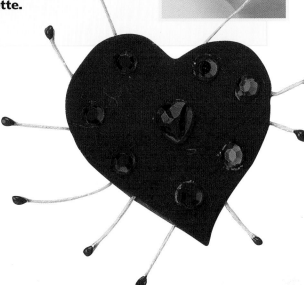

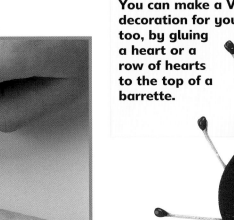

5 To decorate the heart, stick small, red plastic gems or sequins to the front of the brooch using fabric glue. Let the glue dry.

Chocolate lollipops

Why not make these chocolate heart lollipops for all your classmates? Decorate them with Os and Xs so everyone gets a hug or kiss on Valentine's Day!

YOU WILL NEED

4oz (100g) white cooking chocolate

4oz (100g) milk cooking chocolate

lollipop sticks

microwaveable plastic bags

pink and yellow writing icing

baking paper

tray

pencil

scissors

1 Line a tray with baking paper, and draw on hearts with a pencil—leave room below each heart for a lollipop stick. Then turn the baking paper over so that the pencil lines are on the other side. Place the lollipop sticks over the tips of the hearts.

28

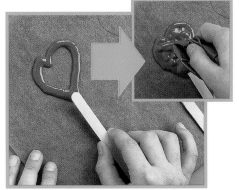

2 Break up the chocolate, and put it into a microwaveable plastic bag. Seal the bag, and put it in the microwave for 30 seconds. If the chocolate has not melted, put it in for another 20 seconds.

3 Let the chocolate cool slightly. Then snip a hole in one corner of the bag. Squeeze out chocolate, following the heart outline.

4 Place the lollipop stick on the chocolate trail. Then fill in the heart with chocolate, covering the top of the stick. Put the lollipops in the fridge to cool and harden. Make some white chocolate lollipops in the same way.

Ask an adult to help you use the microwave.

5 When the lollipops are hard, decorate each one with a heart, a hug, or a kiss using writing icing.

Patterns

Here are the patterns you will need to make some of the projects. To find out how to make a pattern, follow the instructions in the "Making patterns" box on page 5. Some of the patterns are half patterns. There are instructions to help you use the half patterns in the steps for the project.

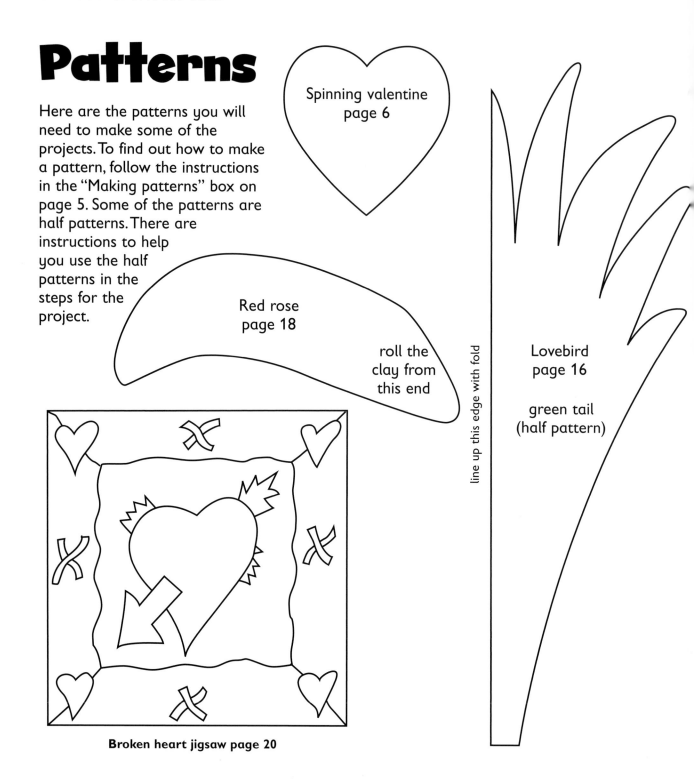

Spinning valentine
page 6

Red rose
page 18

roll the clay from this end

line up this edge with fold

Lovebird
page 16

green tail
(half pattern)

Broken heart jigsaw page 20

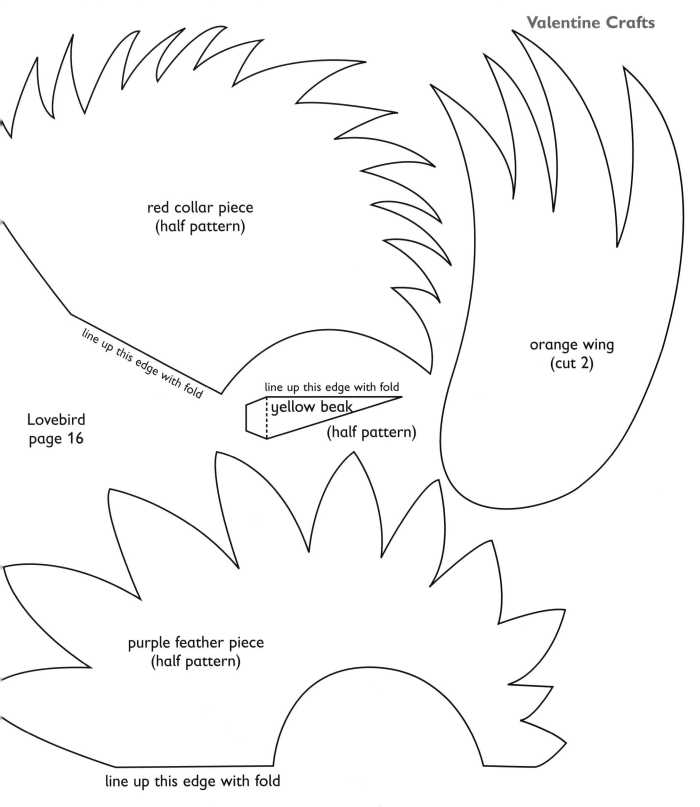

red collar piece
(half pattern)

line up this edge with fold

Lovebird
page 16

line up this edge with fold
yellow beak
(half pattern)

orange wing
(cut 2)

purple feather piece
(half pattern)

line up this edge with fold

Glossary

barrette a clasp used to keep hair in place

brooch a piece of jewelry that is fastened to clothing by a pin

cellophane a thin, transparent, waterproof material used for wrapping and covering

contraption a device or machine

corrugated folded into parallel ridges

initial the first letter of a name

pendant a piece of jewelry that hangs from a necklace

stamen an organ of a flower, usually consisting of a stalk and the part of the flower that produces pollen

tassel a bunch of loose threads tied together at one end that is used as decoration

template a pattern from which similar things can be made

tinsel a thin strip of glittering foil, paper, or plastic used for decoration

varnish a substance that gives an object a protective gloss, or the act of applying this substance

Index

B
Broken heart jigsaw 20–21

C
candy and chocolate projects 12–13, 24–25, 28–29
card ideas 6–7, 8–9, 20–21
Chocolate lollipops 28–29

D
decorations 16–17, 18–19, 22–23, 26–27

F
Fortuneteller 10–11

G
games 10–11, 14–15, 20–21
gift ideas 16–17, 18–19, 22–23, 26–27, 28–29

H
Heart cookies 24–25

J
jewelry ideas 26–27

K
Keepsakes 26–27
Kiss seal 8–9

L
Lavender heart 22–23
Lip smackers 14–15

Lovebird 16–17
Love bugs 12–13

M
materials 4–5

P
patterns 30–31
    how to use 5

R
Red rose 18–19

S
safety guidelines 5
Spinning valentine 6–7

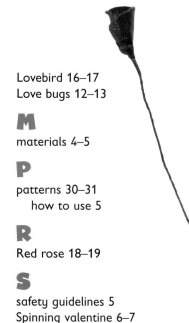